P9-DDC-486

Rank does not
confer privilege
or give power.
It imposes
RESPONSIBILITY.

~ Peter Drucker ~

Start RIGHT,
Stay RIGHT...

LEAD
RIGHT

Every Leader's
Straight-Talk Guide
to JOB SUCCESS

STEVE VENTURA

WALKTHETALK.COM

Resources for Personal and Professional Success

To order additional copies of this handbook, or for information on
other WALK THE TALK® products and services,
contact us at
1.888.822.9255
or visit
www.walkthetalk.com

Start RIGHT, Stay RIGHT... **LEAD RIGHT**

© 2008 Steve Ventura
No part of this book may be reproduced in any form without written permission from the publisher.
International rights and foreign translations are available only through negotiation of a licensing agreement
with the publisher. Inquiries regarding permission for use of the material contained in this book should be
addressed to:

The WALK THE TALK Company
1100 Parker Square, Suite 250
Flower Mound, Texas 75028
972.899.8300

WALK THE TALK books may be purchased for educational, business, or sales promotion use.

WALK THE TALK®, The WALK THE TALK® Company, and walkthetalk.com® are registered trademarks
of Performance Systems Corporation.

Printed in the United States of America

10 9 8 7 6 5 4 3 2 1

Edited by Michelle Sedas
Designed by Steve Ventura
Printed by MultiAd

ISBN-13: 978-1-885228-86-4
ISBN-10: 1-885228-86-4

Contents

As you read this book you'll come across our **Solution Finder!**
Visit WalkTheTalk.com where you can immediately access our
free tips to help you achieve personal and professional success!

INTRODUCTION

You have a title.
Do your people have a leader?

Fact is, having a leadership position and being a leader are not one and the same. Your position is something that was bestowed on you ... something you were appointed to ... something you became eligible for by being a good performer in the past. What you did "yesterday," as an employee, helped you get the title or classification you hold today. And that's exactly what your position is: a title ... a classification.

Being a true **leader**, however, is much different. "Leader" is a descriptor – a label that you EARN through specific behaviors. It's based on what you do *today*, and what you will do *tomorrow* – not what's printed on your business card or engraved on your name tag. And earning the label of "leader" requires that you think and act in ways that are considerably <u>different</u> from what you did before you were promoted. Simply put,

in order to be a leader, you must do the things that leaders do ... and you must do them well.

What are those things? You're about to find out.

Whether you're a seasoned manager or someone just starting in a leadership position, no matter if this is your ideal job or merely one stop on a larger career journey, you need to be successful. This book will show you how! So, pay attention to what you're about to read.

◆ You owe it to your organization – the one that has given a vote of confidence by placing you in your current position ... the one that entrusted you with its most valuable resource: its people.
◆ You owe it to your team members – those who depend on you for leadership and guidance ... those whose performance and results are inextricably linked to yours.

Most importantly ...

◆ You owe it to yourself – the one who must live with the image you see in the mirror ... the one who ultimately benefits from, or is hurt by, the actions you take and the track record you add to each day.

On the pages that follow, you'll find twenty-six "To Do's" – a collection of ideas and proven strategies guaranteed to help you get the results you want and need. They're written in a "pull no punches" style, so get ready for some straight talk.

USE and APPLY the information in this handbook, and you'll not only improve your overall effectiveness, but you'll also build a reputation (and a legacy) as a top-notch leader – someone who will always ...

LEAD RIGHT!

LEADERSHIP
is practiced
not so much in words
as in ATTITUDE …
and in ACTIONS.

~ Harold S. Geneen ~

YOU
and your
MINDSET

Remember the "luxuries" you no longer have.

Why did you go after a management or supervisory position? What attracted you? If you're like most folks, your reasons were probably based around the word "more" – as in *more* money ... *more* prestige ... *more* power, authority, and control ... *more* career opportunities ... *more* privileges ... *more* involvement ... and maybe even *more* responsibility and ability to contribute. In all likelihood, you viewed your promotion in terms of what you would GAIN.

Undoubtedly, you now enjoy a few more "perks" than you did when you were a non-management individual contributor. (If you ever forget what they are, just ask your employees. They can list several things you "get," – or "get to do" – that they don't!) Those benefits compensate for the additional responsibilities and requirements that came with the leadership "territory." You expected to GAIN ... and gain you did.

But guess what? When you joined the ranks of management and super-vision, you also LOST! You lost several "luxuries" – ways of thinking and acting that only non-leaders can exercise and enjoy.

You'll find a list of those lost luxuries on the following page. Review them. Remember them. APPLY them! The mindsets and behaviors they represent are the essence of leadership. More than anything else, they are what separate leaders from followers ... they are what separate poor leaders from great ones.

LOST "LUXURIES"

As a leader, you no longer have the luxury of ...

... thinking mostly about yourself – putting your own needs first.

... acting on feelings rather than facts – jumping to conclusions and reacting in a "knee jerk" fashion.

... whining to others or commiserating with their discontent.

... forming opinions and making judgments knowing only "one side of the story."

... continually blaming "them" and "they" – and expecting someone else to fix what's broken.

... not listening to others' ideas, concerns, and opinions.

... taking sides, overtly favoring some people, and excluding others.

... wearing your emotions "on your sleeve."

And, as a leader, you no longer have the luxury of ...

... closing your eyes or walking away when things happen that just aren't right.

Accept that your "results" now come through others.

E ver stop to think about why your organization placed you in a leadership position? Undoubtedly, it had something to do with you being really good at what you did as an employee ... as an "individual contributor." And that's something you should be very proud of. But that was "then"! Now, your job is much different. Like it or not, now you have a new set of responsibilities to meet, a new list of expectations to satisfy, and a new definition of success to pursue.

As a leader, your primary job is not to "do the work," but rather to direct, encourage, support, and develop *the people* who do the work. Their successes are your successes ... and their failures are yours as well. You'll no longer be judged merely by what you accomplish individually. Your satisfaction must come – and your reputation must be built – on what your people achieve. You shine when THEY are the ones in the spotlight.

So, **make sure your focus and attention are on your team members instead of yourself.** Have a big ego? Find that difficult to swallow? Take a big gulp! Bottom line: Those who can't accept that reality shouldn't accept the additional money that comes with their leadership positions.

> **When the best leader's work is done,
> the people say "we did it ourselves."**
>
> ~ Lao Tzu ~

Be a LEADER – not a "boss" nor a "pal."

Ⲟne of the many things I've learned over the years is that most leadership "wounds" (problems) are self-inflicted. After all, supervisors are human … they aren't perfect … sometimes they shoot themselves in the feet. And of all the mistakes they make, two stand out as the most common and the most problematic.

The first mistake is relying almost entirely on **authority and control** to get the job done – telling employees what to do and looking over their shoulders to make sure they do it. Described conversationally, it's "I talk, you listen … I direct, you comply." Described attitudinally, it's *I'm the boss*. No matter how you describe it, IT'S A PROBLEM! Why? Because most employees don't like being bossed around. They resent it and they resent you for doing it. Worse yet, authoritarian approaches typically stifle team member initiative, creativity, commitment, and satisfaction. Eventually, employees turn off. Some quit and leave … others quit and stay. Either way, you're toast!

The second supervisory mistake is the opposite extreme of the first – being (or trying to be) "one of the guys" and then trading on **friendship** in order to get the job done. What's wrong with that? Lots of things – including the increased potential for favoritism and loss of objectivity when dealing with issues and problems. Then, there's the blurring of your role and authority – which leaves team members with the task of figuring out which "hat" (friend or supervisor) you're wearing at any given moment. Finally, there's the reality that it's just plain tough to manage your buddies. Too often you end up having to choose between doing your job and keeping a friend. Either way, you lose!

So, here's the deal in a nutshell: Your people don't want a "boss" and they undoubtedly have more than enough friends. If you're looking to get the most and best from your group, don't be a dictator or a chum, be a LEADER – someone who motivates, inspires, and models top-notch performance and conduct.

Does that mean you shouldn't give assignments or hold people accountable for their performance and results? No, it doesn't. Does it mean you can't have positive and friendly relationships with the members of your team? No, again. What it means is that your primary mission is enabling and empowering your people to succeed.

How do you do that? Keep reading!

The boss drives people; the leader coaches them.
The boss depends on authority; the leader on good will.
The boss inspires fear; the leader inspires enthusiasm.
The boss says "I"; the leader says "WE."
The boss fixes the blame for the breakdown;
the leader fixes the breakdown.
The boss says "Go"; the leader says "LET'S Go!"

~ H. Gordon Selfridge ~

YOU
and your
PEOPLE

(Employees / Team Members)

Clarify your expectations ...
and *theirs*.

Want to increase the chances that employees will deliver the performance you're looking for? **Tell them what you expect!** Sit down with each of your team members and describe – in specific, behavioral terms – what they need to do to be successful in your eyes.

Seems like a "no brainer" ... right? Sure. But there are still plenty of managers out there who have never taken the time to clarify their performance expectations – rationalizing that lack of communication with statements such as: "It's on the job description" ... "They've been here long enough – they oughtta know by now" ... "They'll figure it out just like I did." In effect, the position each of those managers has taken is:

I expect my people to do what it is I haven't told them.

That's unfair (not to mention STUPID!). So, make sure that shoe doesn't fit you. If it does, stop wearing it. Throw it away! It's got a bullet hole in it!

And while we're on the subject ...

Don't forget to ask your people what it is they need and want from YOU. After all, employees have expectations, too. And they're more likely to follow and support leaders who meet those expectations. When they do, YOU WIN!

The art of communication is the language of leadership.
~ James Humes ~

Let them know how they're doing.

It's been said that "feedback is the breakfast of champions." Well, if that's true, then a lot of employees out there are going hungry. And it's time they got fed!

Ask any group of people how often they receive detailed feedback on their performance at work and it's not unusual to hear: "Only at annual review time … or if I really screw up bad." And that's truly unfortunate. It's unfair for those team members who are left in the dark, and it's yet another self-inflicted wound by leaders who are blowing opportunities to help their people achieve and succeed.

The more employees know how they stack up against your expectations, the easier it is for them to keep their performance on track.

That's why providing specific, detailed feedback needs to be an ongoing process rather than a once-a-year "event." Failure to do that makes about as much sense as a professional sports coach telling his or her players: "I'll let you know how you're doing with those plays at the end of the season." Not only would that be a ridiculous thing for a coach to do, it would also be CAREER LIMITING!

Like a little feedback on how well you give feedback? Try this quick exercise:

Take a piece of paper and list the names of all the people on your team. Next to each name, write down the date you last sat down with that person and reviewed how he or she was doing and what this person could do to be even more successful.

Now analyze your results. If you've given each person performance feedback within the last two months, you're doing well (and probably so are your people). Keep it up! But, if it's been over two months for some people – or you can't remember the last time you did it at all – then you're not doing it enough. And that needs to change!

One more thing …

Think about how you would answer if those employees who haven't received regular feedback from you were to ask:

"Why don't you give us feedback more often?"

And see if YOU would buy the answer you give!

Do right by those who do right.

Ever feel unappreciated or under-recognized for the good work you do? *Uh…Hello!* Ever miss opportunities to recognize and thank your people for the good work that they do? *Um…Oops!*

Of course, all of us occasionally feel taken for granted at work. We know firsthand how lousy that feels. And when we fail to give recognition to our employees, we pass along that same lousy feeling. We do it not because we're bad people, but because we're human, and we're busy … because we're working hard to "hold our own" and, in that process, we sometimes lose sight of what's truly important. But as a leader, you have an opportunity to change that. In fact, you have an *obligation* to change that.

When team members do what you want them to do – when they meet your expectations or go above and beyond the call of duty – there ought to be something in it for them. And that something needs to be more than just "continued employment." But for more employees than you might think, the scenario goes like this: Do bad and you get zapped; do well and you get *nothing* – except the chance to come back tomorrow and relive the scenario all over again. Trust me, there are lots of ways to inspire and motivate people, but **that ain't one of them!** Any leader who thinks otherwise is missing the point … and the boat!

Here's the deal: You want employees to meet your performance and behavior expectations, right? Obviously! And when they do, is your job easier and more satisfying? Sure! And, of course, anyone who makes your job easier deserves your appreciation, right? Absolutely! Then why wouldn't you *show* your gratitude to those folks? NO REASON!

Here's one you can take to the bank: Of all the activities you engage in as a leader, "catching people doing things right" – and recognizing them for it – needs to be one of your top priorities.

Whether it's a tangible reward (when appropriate), a special benefit, or just a sincere "thank you," the act of recognizing team members sends two messages: **good performance matters** and **your efforts and contributions are known and appreciated.** You don't have to be a psychologist to know that messages like those can positively affect employee motivation and satisfaction.

That's great news – and it gets better. Here's the kicker: Providing recognition gets you (the leader) more good performance. Why? Because whenever you recognize any behavior, you also *reinforce* it. And, with few exceptions, …

REINFORCED BEHAVIOR IS REPEATED BEHAVIOR!

Clearly, "doing right by those who do right" is a win-win proposition. Why it isn't done more consistently is one of the great mysteries of leadership. Don't let it be a mystery that applies to you!

> There are two things people want more than sex and money: recognition and praise.
>
> ~ Mary Kay Ash ~

A Letter to Every Leader

Dear Leader:

Okay, maybe I've been known to say: "I don't want any pats on the back – just put it in my check." Well, don't believe it. Regardless of how I sometimes may act, I DO care a lot about what you and others think of me and what I do. Recognition is important to me. That's why I value award pins; that's why I display trophies at home; that's why I hang certificates on my wall.

Believe it or not, I'm looking for more from this job than just a paycheck. There's got to be more, 'cause I'm sure not gonna get rich on what I make! What do I want? I want to feel good about myself and the work I do; I want to feel like I'm an important part of this organization. And I tend to gauge my self-worth by others' perceptions … including yours.

I don't expect you to see me as a top-notch performer all the time. No one is. But I do expect to occasionally be recognized for my efforts and contributions. And the more you recognize my good work, the more good work I want to do. That's "human nature."

I know you're often so busy you probably don't think about recognizing me. And maybe you sometimes figure that you don't get recognition yourself, so why should you give it to others? But if you'll just make a greater effort to let me know you appreciate me, I'll do my best to return the favor. And I promise I won't complain about receiving too much praise!

Every Employee

Adapted from *Walk Awhile In MY Shoes* by Eric Harvey and Steve Ventura
www.walkthetalk.com

Give them a voice ...
and a say.

"**I** wish employees would take more ownership of what we do around here." "They need to look at this as more than just a job." "If only my people would act more like partners in this business."

Sound familiar? Those are fairly common management laments. And chances are you've thought or said them yourself at one time or another. You may even be thinking them right now. If so, I've got good news for you – you're about to become privy to a not-so-secret secret that will serve you well throughout your leadership career. And here it is: If you want employees to act like partners in the business, TREAT THEM LIKE PARTNERS!

If you're thinking that's no big revelation, you're right. It's just common sense. People tend to act according to how they're treated ... according to what they perceive they ARE. Expect employees to check their brains at the door when they come in, and that's just what they'll do – they'll respond as mere "cogs in a wheel." But, give them more of "a voice and a say" in your operation, and they'll take more ownership of it. It IS just that simple.

Giving employees **a voice** means fostering a workplace in which each team member's ideas and concerns are welcomed, considered, and appreciated. It's about taking full advantage of the brainpower existing within your group. And it all starts with four small, yet unbelievably powerful, words – the same ones you wanted to hear when you were an individual contributor:

"What do YOU think?"

Giving employees **a say** means allowing team members to make work-related decisions whenever appropriate and practical. It's about delegating authority along with responsibility ... about taking participation to the next level (beyond just providing input) ... about communicating goals and parameters – and then uttering four more powerful words:

"YOU make the call."

And, it's about understanding and accepting two facts of business life: 1) As a leader, you WILL always be responsible for ensuring that the best decisions are made, and 2) You WON'T always be the best person to make those decisions.

So, look for opportunities to give your team members more of a voice and a say in your operation. You'll end up with more ideas and better decisions. You'll help your people learn and grow. You'll build employee confidence and increase their job satisfaction. And, since people tend to support that which they influence and help to create, you'll likely experience greater team member commitment to the tasks at hand ... and to you. What's wrong with that picture? Absolutely NOTHING!

Explain "why's" as well as "what's."

Chances are you heard it as a kid. Maybe you've even said it, yourself, as a parent. It's that all-too-common response to children who – after being told to do something – ask, "Why do I have to?" And it goes like this: **"Because I said so!"**

Well, guess what? That response isn't restricted to dealings with children. It can (and often does) apply to how leaders interact with their team members at work. Certainly, it's hard to imagine employees actually asking, "Why do I have to?" Nevertheless, when we tell our people *what* to do without explaining *why* it needs to be done, we are – in effect – saying: "Do it because I'm telling you to." And that message is a HUGE turnoff for adults.

So, why do some leaders give instructions and assignments, establish rules and procedures, or require certain changes without communicating the reasons behind them? Here are a few possible explanations ... along with some personal commentary:

1. *They feel that having to "justify" needs and requirements in some way diminishes their authority.*

   Bogus thinking! It's not about justifying, it's about explaining ... about sharing information. A shortsighted "boss" might believe that with-holding information is the key to maintaining authority – a true "leader" would never entertain such irrational thoughts.

2. *They don't believe that employees understanding the reasons for instructions and requirements is important ... or that it will make a difference in the outcome.*

   Nothing could be further from the truth! It's VERY important for your people to know why things need to be done. It helps them feel like valued members of the organization. And when the why's make good sense (which they usually do), it increases employee commitment and dedication to doing what needs to be done.

3. *They don't understand the reasons, themselves.*

   A common problem ... and a lousy excuse! Leaders who don't know why things must be done need to FIND OUT. They need to ask, probe, and dig until they get an answer – and then they need to share that information with their people. What if they can't get that answer? Then they'll know, firsthand, how bad their team members are going to feel.

Bottom line: Unless it will violate a legitimate need for confidentiality, always tell your people the reasons for assignments, instructions, and required changes. That's your WHAT. Your WHY? Because it's how you lead adults, it produces positive results, and it's simply the right thing to do.

Guru:
"Always tell people WHY they should do things."
Student:
"Give me the reason and I will do as you wish."
Guru:
"My point, exactly."

Ask them how *you're* doing.

Finding out what you do well so you can keep on doing it … pinpointing what you don't do so well so you can make the appropriate changes. That's the purpose of performance feedback – something we identified several pages earlier as being critical to employee success. And it's something that YOU need just as much as your people do – for the exact same reasons.

To be sure, you need to know how you're doing as a manager or supervisor … how well you're handling the duties and responsibilities that you'd find on a job description for your position. And you rely on *your* manager to provide that information. But that's not the only feedback you need. You also need to know how you're doing as a LEADER. And the absolute best sources of that information are your people. So, ASK THEM! Just be sure to ask them the right way.

What's the right way? Well, it isn't asking the direct question: "How am I doing as a leader?" All you're likely to get with that type of inquiry is a "Just fine" or "Not bad" response which may stroke your ego but doesn't tell you squat. A better approach is to ask an open-ended question that invites team members to share their true feelings in a way that provides you with useful, constructive information:

> "What one or two things can I do, or stop doing, that
> would make me a better leader in your eyes?"

After asking that question, there are only two things left to do: thank each team member for his or her input *and* ACT ON WHAT YOU HEAR!

Deal with performance problems early.

Hate the thought of dealing with employee performance problems? You've got plenty of company. Most leaders agree that it's the absolute worst part of their jobs.

Having to look someone in the eye and tell them they're not cutting it ranks right up there with getting a root canal. And because it's so unpleasant, you may be tempted to "look the other way" until either the problem goes away on its own (which rarely to never happens) or it becomes so serious and impacting that you have no choice but to act. Don't succumb to that temptation! It's one of the most unfair things you could do to any team member.

As a leader, your job is to help, guide, and motivate employees to be as successful as they can possibly be. And knowing that someone has a performance problem – but saying or doing nothing about it – is NOT the way you meet that responsibility. There are just no valid excuses for inaction on your part.

Think about it. You finally talk with a team member about a problem that has become serious over time. He or she asks how long you've known there was an issue. You answer, "For quite some time now." He or she then asks why you didn't say something sooner. How are you going to respond … what are you going to say? "I was too busy"? "It wasn't a real problem before"? That just won't fly!

So, make and take the time to deal with performance discrepancies as soon as you become aware of them. Work through any fear, anxiety, or discomfort you may have. Fact is, the earlier you address issues, the easier and less emotional they will be to handle ... for everyone involved.

Watch for indicators that an employee may be heading for trouble. The minute you see any, put on your "coaching" hat. Help the person recognize the performance pitfalls *before* sliding down the "slippery slope."

Isn't that what you expect of *your* leader?

> **The best way to escape from a problem is to SOLVE it!**
>
> ~ Alan Saporta ~

FREE ... Performance Problem Discussion
Preparation Checklist
Go to www.walkthetalk.com

Safe Assumptions

Most people realize that making assumptions is bad and can get you into serious trouble. As the saying goes: "When you ASSUME, you make an ASS of U and ME." Nevertheless, as humans we all tend to make them. So here are some safe ones ... things you can feel okay in assuming as a leader:

◆ The e-mails you send will be seen by more people than those they're addressed to.

◆ Things said "just between you and me" won't stay that way.

◆ In all of your dealings with people, what goes around WILL come around – back at you.

◆ Your employees cannot read your mind.

◆ Problems you choose to avoid will usually get worse.

◆ "As long as you don't hear from me, you'll know you're doing okay" is just not true.

◆ Treat one team member poorly, and ten people will hear about it – including your boss ... and Employee Relations.

◆ Your ability to get another leadership position will be directly related to how well you do on the job you have now.

◆ Whenever you think "no one will know," someone will.

◆ Whenever you think "no one cares," someone does.

◆ Whenever you think you're as good as you need to be, YOU AREN'T!

Make sure they have the "tools" they need.

Imagine this scenario: We're out in the middle of a field. I'm the supervisor and I give you an assignment to dig a trench. After explaining why the trench is necessary, I give you the go-ahead to start digging. You inquire, "Where's the back hoe?" I respond, "It's in the shop." You then ask, "So how am I supposed to dig this trench?" I hand you a shovel, and then I leave. I return two hours later and find that you haven't made much progress. You're tired and frustrated … and I'm ticked off.

A far-fetched story? Maybe so. But it does make a simple and important point: it's tough for people to do a good job – to do their best work – when they don't have the "tools" (resources) they need. That's something your team members may be facing more often than you think. And as a leader, you need to do your best to do something about it.

Ask yourself, *What do my people need in order to meet or exceed my expectations?* Better yet, ASK THEM! Maybe it's a new piece of equipment – or the fixing or updating of an existing one. Perhaps it's a new software program, additional training, or an expanded supplies inventory. Or it could be that what they really need is more time, more help, or more information. Whatever your team needs, get it for them. And if you can't, tell them why, look for other ways to support their efforts, and appreciate the fact that many of their achievements are happening in spite of how they are equipped, rather than because of it.

Respect their time.

It's true confession time. Do you typically expect employees to stop whatever they're doing whenever you come to them with a need, a want, or some other item on *your* agenda? Do you ever conduct meetings that are less-than-productive due to a lack of planning or organization on your part? If you answered *yes* to either (or both) of those questions, I've got three words for you: STOP DOING IT! You're wasting one of the most precious resources your people have: their time.

I know, I know. Of course there will be occasions when you have a truly pressing ("legitimate") need that must be addressed immediately. But far too often, leaders interrupt employees with issues that aren't all that significant or important – merely because they want to deal with them NOW and get them off *their* plates. That's just plain inconsiderate. And when it comes to unnecessary or poorly organized meetings in which little is accomplished – well, there's simply no excuse for those, period.

Your people have important work to do. If they didn't, they wouldn't be there. So, make sure your meetings are necessary and well-managed. And, the next time you feel the need to interrupt someone's activities, focus, and concentration, ask yourself: *Is my issue really more important than what he or she is doing right now?* If it is, proceed – if it isn't, wait … and schedule a more appropriate and convenient opportunity to chat.

Bottom line: if you don't respect your people's time, eventually they won't either. Then, everyone loses.

Help them deal with change.

Whether it be in the form of yet another revised policy or procedure to adopt, a new product to make and sell, the latest technology upgrade to learn, a corporate restructuring to figure out (and survive), a new set of job duties to make "happen" – or one of a myriad of other possibilities – continual change is a reality of business life. And it can be a *painful* reality for many people – including the folks who report to us.

Certainly, as leaders, we also are subject to change. And we're not exempt from the discomfort that comes with it. But we have to get past that … we need to "suck it up." We have to focus on our people (rather than ourselves) and be sensitive to their fears, concerns, and needs about stepping out of their "comfort zones." Ultimately, we must be facilitators of change – not dictators, nor mere messengers, nor "victims" of it, ourselves. That is what leadership is all about … that's part of the heat that comes with our leadership kitchens.

HOW TO HELP EMPLOYEES DEAL WITH CHANGE

1. Explain WHY the change is required or necessary.
2. Describe the expected benefits to be gained ("What's in it for us").
3. Provide training and resources necessary to implement the change.
4. Solicit or address any employee questions and concerns.
5. Be patient – expect mistakes as new habits are formed.
And most importantly …
6. Demonstrate support and commitment to the change, yourself.

Nip conflicts in the bud.

Wherever there are people working together, there *will* be tension. Count on it. Expect it. Sooner or later, it's going to happen – a conflict will surface between two or more of your team members. Perhaps you'll see it in their behaviors; maybe someone else on the team will clue you in. How you find out about it doesn't matter. What *does* matter is what you do about it.

Time out! What's the big deal? So some team members are having a spat. That's natural. Just let it be and things will eventually smooth out on their own … right? WRONG! Unlike fine wine, **conflicts that are left alone rarely improve with age.** They're much more likely to fester and decay. Sure, we can ignore them – or try to live with them – but the odds are miniscule that they'll evaporate into thin air and then all will be well with the world again.

Okay, maybe so. *But when employees are having a conflict, it's really their problem and their business … right?* WRONG, AGAIN! When two employees are at odds with each other, **the tension and stress of their conflict spills over onto other members of the team as well.** Their coworkers *know* what's going on, they don't want to "take sides" or "walk on eggshells," and they must deal with – and often compensate for – the counterproductive behaviors that typically result from other people's souring relationships. All that makes it difficult for them to do *their* very best work – and, as a leader, that makes dealing with the conflict YOUR BUSINESS!

So, don't allow interpersonal conflicts between team members to fester. Keep your eyes and ears open for potential problems, and get involved. Either meet with the "combatants" individually or bring them together. Explain your concerns and confirm that a problem exists. Describe how others are impacted and clarify your expectation that the parties will work together to resolve the issue. Work with the involved team members to develop action plans, and then follow up to make sure progress is being made.

To be sure, there's a lot more to conflict resolution than merely what's presented here. You'll probably want to "brush up" on some problem-solving techniques by reading material specific to the subject – or by seeking advice and counsel from a colleague who has dealt with similar issues in the past.

Conflicts are workplace obstacles. Don't let them get in the way of your team's success. Dealing with them may not be pleasant. But having to repair the damage they can cause will be even worse.

 **FREE ... Conflict Warning Signs**
Go to www.walkthetalk.com

Be flexible *and* "zero tolerant."

Join in ... you know the song: *You got to know when to hold 'em, know when to fold 'em.* **Know when to stand your ground, know when to bend.** What? Okay, okay – I know that last part is not really how the song goes. It is, however, how effective leadership "goes." And hopefully you'll be reminded of that every time you hear the tune from now on.

The message of the revised song stanza above is both simple and profound – and it's something that good leaders inherently understand: **Sometimes you need to be *flexible* ... sometimes you need to be *rigid* (i.e., "zero tolerant").** There's a right time and a right place for each. It all depends on the issues and circumstances at hand.

Striking an appropriate balance between flexibility and firmness is critical to your success. Trust me – operating at either extreme <u>all the time</u> is NOT the way to enhance your results, your reputation, or your résumé. If hard-nosed close-mindedness is your only "M.O.," you'll eventually lose your people. If "anything goes – nothing's sacred" is your mantra, you'll eventually lose your job. (Either way, they won't be setting a place for you at the *Leadership Hall of Fame* banquet dinner!).

The best rule of thumb:

> **Be flexible whenever you can,
> be firm whenever you must.**

So, what does it mean to be flexible? It means understanding and accepting that there's usually more than one way to accomplish things – and behaving accordingly. It's about being open to new ideas and different approaches. It's about allowing employees some discretion on how they accomplish their work. It's about accommodating team-member needs and reasonable requests when there's no negative impact on the operation. And it's about "going with the flow" whenever issues really aren't that important or methodologies don't matter all that much.

Many times, however, things *do* matter. They matter a lot. And in those circumstances, you'll want to take a more rigid stance. Perhaps it's achieving a critical team goal. Maybe it's about meeting an important deadline. Whatever the issue, your people need to understand that some things are non-negotiable; they need to expect that, occasionally, you're not going to bend.

Of all the things you *won't* bend on, inappropriate behavior needs to be your number one. Some actions are plainly unacceptable and they need to be approached and addressed with the highest form of rigidity: ZERO TOLERANCE. As an authority figure, you have to draw a line in the sand … you must refuse to accept or allow behaviors that conflict with laws, rules, organizational values, or ethical standards. Faced with any, you must act quickly, competently, and in accordance with your organization's guidelines. Do that, and you'll earn the title "leader." Fail to do that, and you'll deserve the title "accomplice."

Staying in Shape

Looking to build or strengthen your Leadership "muscles"?
Here are some exercises ... **TO AVOID:**

Jumping to conclusions

Passing the buck

Grabbing the credit

Throwing your weight around

Stretching the truth

Bending the rules

Breaking your promises

Playing favorites

Stepping on others

Dodging your duty

Running your mouth off

Plugging your ears

Side-stepping problems

Shooting down the organization

Pulling others into your funk

Holding others back

Pressing "my way or the highway"

Just *skating* by

Help them learn and grow.

Prepare yourself for a very important lesson in effective leadership. You'll need a pencil, a sheet of paper, and a green marker. Ready? Here we go: Using the pencil, trace your hand on the blank paper. Next, take the green marker and completely color the image of your thumb. Now look at the paper. Do you see a green thumb? Great ... that's it ... lesson complete.

Okay, maybe that was corny and somewhat lame, but hopefully you got the point. The best leaders are expert gardeners – in a figurative sense. For them, the skills and capabilities of their team members are invaluable seeds to be nurtured and grown. With growth comes strength; with strength comes confidence. And with strength and confidence comes the ability to do more and to do better – and to feel really good about both.

Try doing a quick assessment of your "gardening" prowess. Ask yourself: *What have I done in the past several months to help each of my team members learn and grow?* If you're able to identify specific strategies you've employed, GREAT! Keep on doing what you're doing. But if you're hard-pressed to list interventions on your part – or if, deep down, you're really not satisfied with what you've done – a change is definitely in order. You'll want to ratchet up things like coaching, training, and developmental assignments that expand employee skills and knowledge.

You've heard it before but it bears repeating: The more your people know and are able to do, the more successful they will be. And the more successful *they* are, the more successful (and respected) YOU are!

Be "choosey" about who you hire and promote.

Of all of the functions and activities that fall under the large umbrella of "leadership," nothing – and I do mean **NO**THING – is more important than staffing. But you sure as heck wouldn't know that based on the way hiring and promotions are often handled!

I know, I know. Staffing is a complicated and time-consuming process. And if you're already knee-deep in alligators, filling a new or vacant position can easily be viewed as "just another freakin' thing I have to do this week that I don't have time for!" So, you rush through the steps and activities – grabbing the first warm body that seems okay – rather than devoting the time necessary to identify the best person for the job. As a result, you often find yourself expending inordinate amounts of time down the road fixing "people problems." *Bang* – another self-inflicted wound!

Clearly, **the more effort you put into hiring and promoting, the less effort you'll have to devote to managing the performance and behaviors of the people you bring on.** To paraphrase an old adage: *You can pay in the beginning, or you can pay in the end ... with interest!*

So, take the time to do selection the right way. Make it a thorough pro-cess ... a top priority. And involve others whose opinions and judgments you trust. Not satisfied with the candidates you have? Then "re-post" the job and find more. Not satisfied with the completeness of an interview? Then schedule a second (or even a third) session. Have doubts about a candidate's skills? Arrange for a test. And by all means, don't forget the background checks.

As a leader, it's imperative that you take selection seriously. Remember that your staff can make you … or they can break you. Ultimately you'll have to live with (and deal with) whoever you hire and/or promote.

Find and select the right people for each open position – regardless of how busy you may be at the time. You owe it to your organization. You owe it to your team. You owe it to yourself!

> # When you hire people that are smarter than you are, you prove you are smarter than they are.
>
> ~ R. H. Grant ~

YOU
and your
BEHAVIOR

Set the example ...
and the tone.

LEADING BY EXAMPLE. It's both a management responsibility and a moral obligation. And, it's the most powerful tool in your leadership toolbox.

You have a strong influence on the thoughts and behaviors of your employees – probably much stronger than you think. Regardless of what appears on job descriptions or in employee handbooks, **your behavior is the real performance standard** that team members will follow. They'll rightfully assume that it's okay and appropriate to do whatever you do. Why wouldn't they? So it's critical that you set the proper example and desired tone ... that you model the performance and behavior you expect from others. Do otherwise, and you're a hypocrite. Ouch!

There's no rocket science here – it's pretty simple stuff. Just pretend that everyone on your team is from Missouri ("The SHOW ME State"). From conduct to commitment ... attendance to attitude ... respect to responsibility ... work ethic to ethics at work – SHOW your people what you want them to do. Let employees know that, in order to be successful, all they have to do is play a game. The name of that game is ...

"FOLLOW THE LEADER!"

FREE ... Success-Killing Phrases
(and thoughts) TO AVOID
Go to www.walkthetalk.com

Stay connected and accessible.

Question: What good is a leader who's rarely around, has little contact with team members, and is difficult to reach whenever employees need him or her? Answer: As a leader, NOT MUCH!

Excuse the harshness of that answer, but the simple reality is that you can't lead people *in absentia*. You have to be around them ... you have to be *with* them enough to have a positive impact on their work and their careers. Squash any misguided "there's my people and then there's my job" thoughts you might have. Your people ARE your job. At least they're a big part of your job. And no matter how many additional duties and responsibilities that come your way, you still must strike a balance ... you still need to stay connected and accessible.

So, work on developing the following three habits:

1. Maintain regular (several times each week) contact with every-one on your team – in person, by phone, or by e-mail.
2. Make sure your people have a way to contact you when they feel the need to do so.
3. Return all calls and messages from team members the same day you receive them.

Remember that the very best way to let your people know you're there for them is to actually BE THERE ... for them.

A "Crash Course" on LEADERSHIP

The **10** most important words:
"What can I do to help you be more successful?"

The **9** most important words:
"I need you to do this, and here's why ..."

The **8** most important words:
"That's my mistake and I will fix it."

The **7** most important words:
"My door is always open to you."

The **6** most important words:
"Let's focus on solving the problem."

The **5** most important words:
"You did a great job!"

The **4** most important words:
"What do YOU think?"

The **3** most important words:
"Follow my lead."

The **2** most important words:
"Thank You."

The **MOST** important word:
"YOU"

Keep your commitments.

Dependable. Reliable. Trustworthy. Do those words describe you? If asked, would your team members say that your word is "good as gold"? The answer to each of those questions needs to be a resounding "yes" if you are going to be the kind of leader that others will follow.

All successful leaders place a premium on keeping their promises and commitments. If they say they'll do something – whether "important" or seemingly insignificant – they remember it … and they DO it. They count on the fact that people can count on them. And they understand that statements like …

> *I was gonna,*
> *I meant to,*
> *I haven't forgotten,*
> *I'll get to it soon …*

all translate the same way: **I JUST DIDN'T DO IT!**

Those are excuses. They're close to meaningless. Each time they're uttered, they chip away the trust and confidence employees have for their management. And when those two factors are gone, so is your ability to lead.

The good news: With few exceptions, all leaders really do *intend* to keep "their word" and their promises. The bad news: Good intentions alone won't take you very far. You get no "points" for them. Points come only when you deliver.

So, don't make promises lightly … don't make ones you can't (or really don't intend) to keep … don't mislead the people that ultimately will determine your success. And when you *do* make commitments, write them down, check them frequently, do whatever it takes to make good on them.

Earn the right to expect others to keep *their* word by keeping *yours*.

> **As a leader, your word is only as good as your last promise kept … or broken.**
>
> ~ Barbara "BJ" Gallagher ~

Don't pass the buck ...
or the blame.

Ever had a leader who pointed fingers, blamed others, and displayed a "Hey, don't look at me" attitude? No, you haven't – because true leaders don't practice that garbage. But some "bosses" do. And if you've ever worked for someone like that, you probably remember quite clearly how much respect you DIDN'T have for him or her. Take a lesson from that poor soul – don't follow his or her lead!

If there's any concept that's synonymous with "leadership" it's got to be **responsibility**. And, behaviorally, that translates into OWNERSHIP. To be an effective and respected leader ...

> ... You must *own* (i.e., support and be committed to) your organization's mission, plans, and initiatives.
>
> ... You must *own* all of the duties and responsibilities that come with your job.
>
> ... You must *own* (i.e., be accountable for) the performance and results of your team.
>
> ... You must *own* (i.e., admit to and fix) your personal mistakes and shortcomings.

So, do a little self-reflection. Ask yourself: What am I doing to demonstrate ownership in the four areas mentioned above? Make sure you're assuming the responsibility that is rightfully yours. And the next time you're tempted to pass the buck or the blame, remember this:

**Whenever you point a finger at someone else,
three of your fingers point back ... AT YOU!**

Don't shoot the messenger.

I want everyone to tell me the truth even if it costs them their jobs!
~ Samuel Goldwyn ~

Unless you happen to be a direct descendent of the Grim Reaper, you're probably not overjoyed with the prospect of hearing bad news. Who the heck is? Most of us have plenty of problems to deal with ... more than enough fires to put out. Bring us another issue and we resent it. We resent the problem – and, far too often, we resent the person who tells us about it. So, we respond negatively to the news ... we "shoot the messenger." And we end up "accomplishing" three things:

1. We vent (inappropriately) and temporarily feel better.
2. We punish a team member for doing the right thing.
3. We create an even bigger problem for ourselves.

What's the bigger problem we create? It goes like this: If employees get zapped for telling us about problems, they'll stop telling us. If they don't tell us, we won't know. If we don't know what's broken, we can't fix it. And if we don't fix what's broken, we're not doing our jobs as leaders. Eventually, *we're* the ones who will get zapped! Trust me, in this case ...

IGNORANCE IS NOT BLISS!

So, how do you respond when team members tell you about problems? How would *they* say you respond? If your reaction tends to be cold and negative, target that behavior for immediate change. Don't punish people who bring you bad news. Instead, thank them! They're really doing you a huge favor. It may be a favor in disguise, but it's still a favor.

Embrace diversity.

Ever find yourself thinking that people who are different from you (different skin color, religion, ethnicity, way of speaking, way of thinking, etc.) are strange, wrong, or perhaps something worse (i.e., derogatory)? If so, it's time to unscrew the top of your head, throw out some of the garbage in there, and catch up with the human race – not to mention the laws of our land. There's *no* place for this type of thinking within the ranks of leadership.

Here's the reality: Each of us is unique … no two people are exactly the same. So, if being different equated to being wrong, EVERYONE WOULD BE WRONG – including YOU! That would definitely be bad. But you know what would be worse? If everyone were exactly alike! In that case, we'd all look, sound, and act the same. We'd only need one type of food, one way of thinking, one sport, one channel on our televisions, one kind of music, one make of car, one style of clothes, one political party – simply one of everything.

With everyone the same, we wouldn't have creative "oddballs" inventing new technologies and creature comforts to improve our lives; we wouldn't have "foreigners" buying our products and services; we wouldn't have the blending of cultures and ideas that afford us new and enriching experiences. And you wouldn't have individual employees bringing the varied skills, ideas, and strengths you rely on for your team's (and your) ongoing success.

Of course, there are times when being different IS being wrong. And in those cases, we have laws, rules, and procedures to control inappropriate behavior. Most of the time, however, different isn't wrong – it's just different. And that's a fact that everyone needs to accept. Better yet, that's a fact that everyone needs to embrace. It is, after all, what allows you to be different from someone else ... and to be proud of it!

So, work on maximizing your respect for diversity – and insist that everyone on your team does the same. Appreciate individuals who are "different" – especially those of other races, cultures, creeds, and national origins. It's the legal thing to do ... it's the moral thing to do ... it's the smart thing to do.

> The real death of [this country] will come when everyone is alike.
>
> ~ James T. Ellison ~
> adaptation

WORDS TO LEAD BY ...

Leadership is the art of getting someone else to do something you want done because he wants to do it.
~ Dwight D. Eisenhower ~

Leadership should be born out of the understanding of the needs of those who would be affected by it.
~ Marian Anderson ~

A good leader takes a little more than his share of the blame, a little less than his share of the credit.
~ Arnold H. Glasgow ~

Leaders don't force people to follow – they invite them on a journey.
~ Charles S. Lauer ~

Outstanding leaders go out of the way to boost the self-esteem of their personnel. If people believe in themselves, it's amazing what they can accomplish.
~ Sam Walton ~

The key to successful leadership today is influence, not authority.
~ Ken Blanchard ~

Being powerful is like being a lady. If you have to tell people you are, you aren't.
~ Margaret Thatcher ~

Model the best,
remember the worst.

There's no question that you were exposed to some very powerful lessons on effective leadership prior to turning the first page in this book. Fact is, you received them well before you were promoted to a leadership position. Where did they come from? Well, they came courtesy of all the managers and supervisors you've had throughout your working career.

Think back on all the various people you've worked for. Some you'll remember fondly – some not so fondly. Undoubtedly, some were "saints" … or at least they exhibited almost saintly behaviors. These were top-notch leaders who showed you, by their example, what you should be doing now. Emulate them; follow their lead. When in doubt, ask yourself "What would he do … how would she handle this situation?" Then, DO IT!

Maybe your inventory of past bosses also includes one or two jerks … and you'd probably just as soon forget them. DON'T! You need to remember them clearly and frequently. They provide your best lessons on what NOT to do! By avoiding the kinds of behaviors they exhibited, you'll make sure that, down the road, you never appear on any of your team members' lists of worst leaders.

> **People seldom improve when they have no other model but themselves to copy after.**
>
> ~ Oliver Goldsmith ~

Keep learning and growing, yourself.

From *The Leader's Guide to Stupid Thinking:* "I'm in a leadership position because I've learned everything I need to learn … I've already mastered all the aspects of my job."

Is there *really* a book with that title? Nope! But there ought to be 'cause it's no secret there's plenty to write about! Do people *really* think that they have nothing further to learn? Well, if you examine the behaviors of some managers and supervisors, the answer has to be YES! And that's truly unfortunate. The big question: Are YOU a member of that group?

Once again, it's self-reflection time. Grab a pad and pencil, and make a list of all the things you've done in the last six months to enhance your job knowledge and skills. Then, candidly evaluate your list. Would you feel comfortable showing it to your manager, your colleagues, and your team members as an example of a good continuous-learning plan? Would you submit it as an example of what effective and competent leaders need to do? If *yes* – GREAT … stay at it! If no, NOT GREAT … change it!

Remember: besides developing your people, you also need to develop yourself. So, take full advantage of the leadership development resources (videos, books, seminars, etc.) offered by your organization. Read industry publications. Consider enrolling in classes offered at local colleges. Engage a mentor whom you respect and admire.

When do you reach the point where you know everything you need to know? NEVER!

Perform with ethics and integrity.

Doing what's right. Keeping yourself and your people out of trouble (not to mention jail). Being a role model for appropriate conduct and business practices. Upholding organizational standards. Earning the respect of others. If those things have little meaning to you, then here's a harsh reality: you have no business holding a leadership position! But if they are as important to you as they should be, then it's critical that you behave ethically and perform with a high level of integrity.

Unless you've been stranded on a deserted island for the last several years, you know there are some serious problems out there in the business world. And it's absolutely imperative that you and your organization do not get caught up in them. The stakes are unbelievably high; the tolerance for inappropriate behavior, anywhere, is rapidly becoming ZERO; the need to ensure that people do "the right thing" is universal.

Sure, "ethics" is a huge and complex subject. But truth be told, the number one (and probably most important) key to always doing what's right is actually quite simple:

THINK BEFORE YOU ACT!

(What a novel idea!) That means checking decisions and planned activities to ensure "rightness" *before* implementing them.

Use the questions below – or similar ones supplied by your organization – as your litmus test. Answering "no" or "I don't know" to one or more of these should be your clue(s) that: 1) You need a different approach, or 2) You probably need counsel and advice from your manager – or someone else in a position of authority.

THE ETHICAL ACTION TEST

A. Is it legal?

B. Does it comply with our rules and guidelines?

C. Is it in sync with our organizational values?

D. Will I be comfortable and guilt-free if I do it?

E. Does it match our stated commitments and guarantees?

F. Would I do it to my family or friends?

G. Would I be perfectly okay with someone doing it to me?

H. Would the most ethical person I know do it?

From: Ethics4Everyone: The Handbook for Integrity-Based Business Practices
www.walkthetalk.com

 Solution FINDER

FREE...Ethics Self-Assessment
Go to www.walkthetalk.com

Integrity is not
a 90 percent thing,
not a 95 percent thing;
either you have it
or you don't!

~ Peter Scotese ~

How Successful Am I? A Self-Assessment

Read the statements below. Think about each one, and then respond as honestly as possible.

NO

[N] 1. I place the majority of my focus and attention on my team members rather than on myself and my own needs.

[Y] [N] 2. I make a conscious effort to avoid being "bossy" – and to not use friendship as a strategy for getting things done.

[Y] [N] 3. I understand and accept that I cannot be successful unless my employees are successful.

[Y] [N] 4. I have told each of my team members what I expect of them (in specific terms), and asked them what they expect of me.

[Y] [N] 5. I give my employees specific feedback about their performance on a regular basis.

[Y] [N] 6. I make a special effort to catch employees doing things right – I recognize / reward good performance whenever I see it.

[Y] [N] 7. I regularly ask employees for their thoughts and opinions, and I let them make business decisions whenever appropriate.

[Y] [N] 8. Whenever I give an assignment or communicate a requirement, I always give the reasons behind it ... I explain WHY's as well as WHAT's.

[Y] [N] 9. I periodically ask team members for feedback on MY performance – and I make a sincere effort to act on the information I receive.

[Y] [N] 10. I don't put off dealing with employee performance problems – I always address them as soon as I become aware of them.

[Y] [N] 11. I frequently check with my team members to make sure they have the equipment, resources, and information necessary to do their jobs. I ask them what they need and do my best to get it for them.

[Y] [N] 12. I respect my people's time. I make sure meetings are necessary and productive, and I avoid interrupting employees with issues and needs that really can wait.

[Y] [N] 13. I work with team members to help them deal with change as painlessly as possible – I'm sensitive to their fears and concerns about it.

[Y] [N] 14. Whenever I become aware of interpersonal conflicts between team members, I intervene immediately rather than letting problems fester.

Y N 15. I am flexible and give my people a lot of latitude on how they get things done, but I do not tolerate violations of laws, procedures, or ethical standards.

Y N 16. I have development plans for each of my team members to enhance their knowledge, skills, and confidence. I spend a considerable amount of time helping my people learn and grow.

Y N 17. I take hiring and promotions very seriously. No matter how busy I am, I devote the time and effort necessary to find, and bring on, the very best people.

Y N 18. I am totally committed to "leadership by example." I make a conscious effort to consistently model the behaviors and performance that I expect from everyone on my team.

Y N 19. I maintain regular contact with each of my employees, and I make sure they know how to (and can) reach me if they feel the need.

Y N 20. Whenever I make a promise or a commitment, I remember it … and I KEEP it. For me, it's critical that my word is my bond.

Y N 21. I take full responsibility for myself and my team – and I avoid pointing fingers at others. I admit to my mistakes and I fix them.

Y N 22. I don't shoot messengers. I accept bad news calmly and respectfully – and I appreciate the courage it takes to surface problems.

Y N 23. I value and appreciate people with ideas, backgrounds, and demographic characteristics that are different from my own.

Y N 24. I make a conscious effort to emulate the best leaders I've experienced in my life … and to avoid the behaviors of the worst.

Y N 25. I continually look for – and take advantage of – opportunities to learn and grow, and I avoid "I know all I need to know" thinking.

Y N 26. It's critically important for me to always perform with ethics and integrity … and I do it! I refuse to compromise my standards and values.

Now, go back and highlight each of the statements for which you checked the NO box (there should be some … unless, of course, you're perfect). These are the areas you should work on in order to increase your leadership effectiveness and overall job success. Develop informal action plans, make a personal commitment to see them through, and get started. And for all those that you checked YES: Congratulations … and keep doing what you're doing!

Closing THOUGHTS

To be sure, your past performance as an individual contributor – your "track record" – significantly impacted your eligibility for a management or supervisory position. Being really good at what you did (past tense) helped you get to where you are today.

But your promotion wasn't just a reward for being a good employee. It was a vote of confidence ... a sign that your organization believes you have the ability and potential to be successful in a much different role. The key word there is "different."

Things changed the moment you accepted a LEADERSHIP position.

"The bar" was raised along with (hopefully) your salary. Requirements went up, responsibilities went up, and expectations went up. You're now held to a higher standard – which is exactly as it should be. And that's not all. Along with your new title also came new functions, new tasks, and a new definition of – and pathway to – "success."

Now, you accomplish things through others. Now, the way you make a difference is by helping *your people* make a difference ... helping *them* be successful. Now, you must be as proficient in the business of leadership as you are in the business of your business. And helping *you* do all of that is what this book has been about.

Have the preceding pages covered every aspect and responsibility of being a leader? Of course not! Did I provide everything there is to know about the subject areas addressed? No, again. No publication (or author) could ever accomplish that. What I *have* done is assemble a collection of helpful mindsets and proven strategies – tips and techniques that have been passed on to me, over the years, by the most effective leaders I have ever experienced. Assuming that, like me, you have more things to do than time to do them, I've tried to zero in on the information you need to not only survive, but also succeed in your vital leadership role.

But there is a catch. As written, the strategies presented in this work are just words … only good ideas. **You have to put them into ACTION in order for their value and benefits to be realized.**

So keep this book handy, re-read it periodically, refer to it often. USE this material to help you and your employees achieve the success you want and need. Use this material to help ensure that you …

Start RIGHT, Stay RIGHT … **LEAD RIGHT**

When the leadership is right,
and the time is right,
the people can always
be counted upon
to follow – to the end
at all costs.

~ Harold J. Seymour ~

The Author

STEVE VENTURA is a recognized and respected author, educator, book producer, and award-winning training program designer. His work reflects over thirty years of human resource development experience – both as a practitioner and a business consultant. His prior books include *Start Right ... Stay Right; Five Star Teamwork; Forget for Success; Walk Awhile In My Shoes; What to Do When Conflict Happens; Who Are THEY, Anyway?; Yes Lives in the Land of No* and *Walk The Talk.*

The Publisher

For over thirty years, *WalkTheTalk.com* has been dedicated to one simple goal ... one single mission: *To provide you and your organization with high-impact resources for your personal and professional success.*

We specialize in ...

- ◆ "How To" Handbooks and Support Material
- ◆ Video Training Programs
- ◆ Motivational Newsletters
- ◆ Inspirational Gift Books
- ◆ Do-It-Yourself Resources
- ◆ 360° Feedback Processes
- ◆ The Popular *212° the extra degree, Start Right ... Stay Right,* and *Santa's Leadership Secrets*® Product Lines
- ◆ *And much more!*

Contact The WALK THE TALK Team at
1.888.822.9255

Or visit us at *www.walkthetalk.com*

WALKTHETALK.COM
Resources for Personal and Professional Success

Other Recommended Resources
Lead Right Library

A complete library of 14 best-selling leadership resources! Tackling leadership topics such as coaching, recognition, communication, and ethics, this library contains everything that you need to lead right. Whether you are a senior manager or just starting out your professional career...these books are for you!

Only $99.95 per set!

Start Right...Stay Right
Every Employee's Straight Talk Guide to Job Success

Start Right, Stay Right is a powerful guidebook for ALL employees, regardless of their level, function, or time on the job. Using a straight-talk, real-world approach, it pinpoints the critical behaviors necessary for individual and organizational success. Make a key component of your:

- New-hire orientation programs
- Ongoing employee training
- Leadership development initiatives

This is the handbook you'll want everyone reading and using...**TODAY!**
$12.95 per copy *(quantity discounts available)*

ORDER FORM

www.walkthetalk.com

✓ **Please send me additional copies of LEAD RIGHT**

1-24 copies: $12.95 ea.   25-99 copies: $11.95 ea.   100-499 copies: $10.95 ea.   500+ copies: *Please Call*

LEAD RIGHT _____copies   X $_____   = $_____

Additional Resources

Lead Right Library   _____sets   X $ 99.95   = $_____

Start Right ... Stay Right Handbook   _____copies   X $ 9.95   = $_____

	Product Total	$_____
	*Shipping & Handling	$_____
	Subtotal	$_____
	Sales Tax:	
(Sales & Use Tax Collected on TX & CA Customers Only)	TX Sales Tax – 8.25%	$_____
	CA Sales/Use Tax	$_____
	TOTAL (U.S. Dollars Only)	$_____

*Shipping and Handling Charges							
No. of Items	1-4	5-9	10-24	25-49	50-99	100-199	200+
Total Shipping	$6.75	$10.95	$17.95	$26.95	$48.95	$84.95	$89.95+$0.25/book

Call 972.899.8300 for quote if outside continental U.S. Orders are shipped ground delivery 3–5 days.
Next and 2nd business day delivery available – call 1.888.822.9255.

Name_____   Title _____

Organization _____

Shipping Address _____
        No P.O. Boxes

City_____ State_____ Zip _____

Phone _____ Fax _____

E-Mail_____

Charge Your Order: ❏ MasterCard   ❏ Visa   ❏ American Express

Credit Card Number_____ Exp. _____

❏ Check Enclosed (Payable to: WalkTheTalk.com)

❏ Please Invoice (Orders over $250 ONLY) P.O. # (required) _____

Prices effective January, 2008 are subject to change.

PHONE	**ONLINE**	**MAIL**
1.888.822.9255	www.walkthetalk.com	WalkTheTalk.com
or 972.899.8300	**FAX**	1100 Parker Square, Suite 250
M-F, 8:30 – 5:00 Central	**972.899.9291**	Flower Mound, TX 75028

WALKTHETALK.COM

Resources for Personal and Professional Success